Echoes That Bloom

Foreword by Joey Guerra

Scott Moore

DAXSON PUBLISHING

Echoes that Bloom
© 2026 Scott Moore
ISBN: 978-1-966337-29-4
Library of Congress control number: 2026900934

Cover art
© 2025, Emerson Guerra-Moore

First Edition, 2026

Printed in the United States of America

Edited by Cherice Cameron and Rachel Cartwright
Cover Design by Lauren Belcher
Layout Design by Kallie Hunchman

Dedicated to my husband and son:
Joey Guerra, Jr., and Emerson Guerra-Moore.
I love you both more than you will ever know.

ECHOES THAT BLOOM
Scott Moore

CONTENTS

Seedling...

In the Beginning • 17
The Roads, The River, The Revival Tent • 18
My First Trip to a Library • 20
We Were Brothers Then • 22
The Visiting Preacher and the Prayer Line • 23
Springfield, MO • 25

The Soil is Fertile...

Always on My Way Back Home • 31
The Death of St Louis • 32
Before God, (an Orchestrated Rebellion in Two Parts) • 35
January 13, 1985 • 37
One Hard Night • 38
Still • 39
Restless in the Heat • 40
Living Crucifixion • 41
Ritual • 42
The Last Day of Us as a Couple • 43

Where Did the Flowers Go...

The Wise Man Built His House • 49
There is Something Beautiful in a Storm Whether Coming or
Going (an Elegy for Ken) • 50
We Are, We Were... Transubstantiation
(an Elegy for Ken) • 52
In the Three Years I Called You My Lover
(an Elegy for Husaini) • 55
The Things I Can't Forget, Things I Can't Keep
(an Elegy for Joe) • 60
The Things That Are Held in the Heart of the Earth
(an Elegy for Michael) • 61
After You Died I Drove to New Orleans to Hide (for Ken) • 62
An Elegy for Joe Perez •
When We Were Vampires at Night (an Elegy for Michael) • 66
The Things That God Holds Above Us
(an Elegy for Michael) • 68
The Elegy for the Lover Who Isn't Dead • 71

Let it Sleep (an Elegy for Michael) • 72
I Step Over Magnolia Blossoms When They Have
Fallen to the Ground • 73
You Gave Them To Me in My Hand (an Elegy for Ken) • 75
This is for When I Crave the Smell of Moist Soil
(an Elegy for Tracy Karl Silverberg) • 77
Our Last Date Before You Died
(an Elegy for Ken) • 78

The Apples Have Fallen From the Trees...

Mom and Dad • 83
A Room With No Doors (an elegy in 5 parts for my father - The
Rev. Denver Moore) • 84
Kinder Than the Man (an Elegy for my Mother) • 89

Echoes Will Bloom...

When Life Offers a Healing • 95
The Disturbing Tale of the Dancing Pig
(A Tribute to Kenny Joe Spivey) • 96
The Fog Lies Against the Horizon • 98
Last Night • 99
At Work • 100
Is This How You Settle Down • 101
Zoom Therapy • 102
Traces • 103
It Is All I Have Left at the End of the Day
(For Emerson) • 104
You and I: A Poem for my Son • 105
Today I'm Dad • 106
March 22, 2025 • 107
Can a Pig Just be Free (The Pigs Dance II) • 108

Foreword

I've always known Scott was a poet, even if he forgot a few times along the way.

When we first met — it shocks me to say three decades ago — he'd often surprise me with poems. The way he used language was different from anything I'd read in school. His words were vibrant and sensual, full of emotion and angst. It was new and exciting. He wrote a poem for me on a large, brown leaf that I framed alongside a photo. He wrote out the lyrics to the song "Sweet Darlin'" by Heart and mailed them to me at home. Not his own words, but poetic in its own way.

Over the years, Scott the poet was set aside for Scott the boyfriend, Scott the professional, Scott the husband, Scott the dad. But he was still there, scribbled on scraps of paper and scuttled away in boxes. Seeing him reawaken in the past year has made my heart swell. Watching him put together this collection, with so much love and investment, has made me incredibly proud. Reading his words, and watching audiences react so viscerally during readings, has filled me with gratitude and awe.

As a music critic for the Houston Chronicle, one of the largest and most influential news sources in Texas, I try to create my own poetry with words. What Scott does is wholly, and beautifully, different. Every line transmits a feeling. Every phrase is tied to a memory. Every break carries its own weight of meaning. His words about his mother and father and past relationships are like a glimpse into the deepest reaches of his soul.

Most importantly, watching Scott's evolution as a poet and reading this book has shown me that poetry is all around us, from the crackle of gravel under a car tire to the flick of a light switch. We just have to find it and hold on.

Joey Guerra

Preface

This book is a love letter—it isn't just written in ink, but in memory, in sin and flesh, in blood. It is a memoir told through poetry, shaped by the enduring, imperfect, and healing power of love.

Love has followed me through every chapter of my life: from the tender, sometimes misguided efforts of my parents to raise me in forgiveness and hope shrouded in religious fervor, to the men who offered sanctuary as I stepped away from the spiritually zealous upbringing and into the hedonistic strains of adulthood. Love not only lives in the haunting echoes of young lives lost too soon, but also in the quiet strength of my husband, and in the boundless wonder of my son.

Not only a tribute to people, but these poems are also rooted in the places that held and nurtured me—beneath the silver legs of the St. Louis Arch, lost in the jubilant pulse of New Orleans jazz, and finally, cradled in the humid arms of Houston heat. The DNA of each city taught me something special about love: how it can be overbearing, spontaneous, grounding, and redemptive.

Life doesn't explain itself. It hands us moments—some luminous, some painful—and asks us to find our own meaning. This collection is my attempt. A gathering of experiences that have carved deep canyons inside of me, yet continue to echo and fill those canyons with warmth and humanity.

In this landscape, with these characters, love is not perfect. But it is real. And it lasts.

Seedling…

In the Beginning....

Sunset fell in shades of purple and red
And here in the hot St. Louis twilight
Mississippi water and flower bed
Your birth lit up the stagnant July night

Full body warm with your fresh fleshy skin
A mother and infant at their first pluck
Swaddled by breast flower and sweet rose scent
Innocence shared between nipple and suck

A pure white dove ascends from river mud
You will soon spread your wings and fly away
From your home nestled in current and flood
Find strength in the sun of a summer day

A mother's prayer for your soul to keep
I can force myself at last to sleep

The Roads, The River, The Revival Tent

in this dusty delta town
        miles close to the open mouth
                of the massive mississippi
river mud cakes the bottom of
        the white frame houses
                propped up on cinder blocks
the gravel roads snake
        crackle and cry beneath car tires
                leaving behind a gust of gray grime
and fans–
        window fans
                attic fans,
                        ceiling fans
                                and handheld fans
futile–
nothing dares move this air
during the day
        denizens of this town
                shuffle through errands
                        pale prisoners of their own choices
but as the sun pushes against
        a pillow of damp towards the west
                this is a haven
                        a small hamlet with a loud heartbeat
and here beneath a giant tarp
        stretched over a field of dust and clover
                you gingerly lay me on the dirt floor
                      next to your purse
beneath a row of folding chairs
        covered by a huge tarp
                you prepare your walk
                      with a handkerchief and a hymnal
down to an altar humid with weeping and tears
        guttural moans
                a crestfallen howl
i want to rescue you from here
        from this ninety-degree sandlot

of high-neck collars
                mid-calf hems and long sleeves.
from here
        where the kicked up dust
                and washed up mud
                        tattoos itself on your soul
from here where
        the roads are weak
                the river is wild
                        there is no way up but under

My First Trip to a Library

My eyes were as big as a roulette wheel and spinning
There were just so many books   bound volumes
    stacked on shelves and carts   laying on tables
        surrounded by an earnest silence   plush like a pillow
        more joyful than playground laughter

I was seven then and hadn't read much more than a Bible
I pulled out a book about a forest
    kids dropping bread pieces foreboding darkness approaching
        a house you could eat   birds ate the bread pieces
        then a kettle and a wicked….

Too scary—keep looking
the sun was still shining   cold and bright December light
    through a huge wall all glass
        that overlooked an Overland street   dull in concrete gray
           casting a longitudinal   stripe of light
             down the spines of a row of children's books
             illuminating numbers on white strips
             like scribbles I couldn't read

When I sat down on the floor
with a book about a beach and seashells
    a light blue hard cover smelling of browned paper and spine
glue   was a balm   in my suburban Gilead
        that seemed like a wasteland
           repetitive houses   cash lending businesses
I had never been outside of the landlocked midwestern United
States
But here I was
      between colorful pages
        on a beach   warm
          by an ocean   tranquil blue
            on sand   soft and sympathetic

the seashells   singing in my ear
resonating   echo and hum

I don't remember falling asleep on the carpet
I don't remember mom finding me curled up
I always imagined that she didn't want to wake me
disturb the dreams emanating from this new world
that I was so excited to discover

We Were Brothers Then

We stayed up until
Twelve whispering,
Each whisper crisp
Like the yellow
Newspaper comics
We'd cut up and
Paste on the pink
Type-writer sheets
We'd get from dad when
He'd return from work.
This night I was ten
And had never been up
       That late so I was scared.
But the stroke of midnight
Found us on the carpet,
Wedged between
The couch and the picture window
For hours waiting
For the sun and talking.
As the sun came up,
Finally shining on us
We turned thirty
And then eventually sixty.
Those late nights behind the couch
Were replaced by phone calls,
Infrequent and sometimes hurried—
But always treasured.
But we would soon learn
As with all things in life
A reverse option
Is not given
And we would never
Find our way back there.

The Visiting Preacher and the Prayer Line

It's hot.

The red carpet down the center of the room

Is darkened by shoes and soil and

The self-righteous smell of musty sermons and sin

Secretions that seep into the padding on the pews.

We all stand in the center and front,

A cluster of panting and palpitation.

Thin summer dresses and cotton shirts

Stuck by damp skin to legs, buttocks, and belly bulge

You finally get down the line to me,

At fourteen, my sins are more fantasy than fact

But transgression, followed by repentance,

Laced with self-deprecating remorse

Is the only door inside this

World that will lead to heaven.

As this pretense portends my willing guilt and

Your arms spread over me in prayer like the legs of

A thousand men, solemn and sacramental

Your hot breath is in my face. Your face is inches from mine.

The perspiration on your hand

Pastes your palms to my moist temples

And I want to reach up with my tongue

To lick the salt from the tips of your fingers.

I feel drops of your spit on my nose and submit,

As my forehead seizures towards your chin

A trickle of sweat lining down the inside of my pant leg.

I am blood and tissue beneath skin and bone

Heartbeat and hard-on.

As I open my eyes, I see outside through

The tiny clear panes of an otherwise stained-glass window,

    The expanse of nature's creation

    A great tailed grackle

    Perched on a river birch branch

    Inquisitive, suspicious,

    —But as free as God made her—

    Peering at us as we pray.

Springfield, MO

The tile floors of this
gymnasium had never held
any more passion than a
stomping Youth for Christ
rally—and they were hollering
hot tonight. Most of the
senior class showed up—
girls with freckles conspicuously
made over and boys jingling
car keys and pocket change.
"Just As I Am" was all
stress and genitalia as my
mind strayed in and out of the crowd
to where he was,
just a few seats over,
the ass so round
and thighs so firm
that I couldn't look away.

We found a spot,
just over in the gloryland
(next to an old clock tower)
unseen by other teens—
alone on the brick and grass.
And when Heaven started
coming down to dream and wire,
you could fill a hymnal with
the splendor we passed between
us with our tongues. The
dry dust of the plains
mixed with the sweat and
stuck to our bodies—

a thick paste we teased
sweet on our lips.
Then we lay silently next
to the full moon.
A moon as fully naked
as us yet every bit
as fervent in its passion
and unyielding in its determination
as the preacher up on stage.

This Soil is Fertile...

Always on My Way Back Home

always on my way back home
but never quite making it there
because home is so far away
and i'm a wildflower born for something else

wildflowers always find new homes
new fields next to new highways
new feet to trample their blooms
seeds blown by winds on tiny particles of dust

i found my home in the backrooms of bars
in the beds of strange men with familiar ways
but there is comfort in the weeds
and familiarity in a tangle of root and topsoil

i'll live in this twist of seedling and shrub
and rest with flowers that bloom in the night

The Death of St Louis

St. Louis died last night
I think
in bursting thrusting gusts of white
molten lava
        shooting hot from its
tallest most erect building.
The ground
shook and mamma cried over her biscuits
because the gravy's turned white and
she's started into singing out a song
all about grandfather's clock
too large for the shelf
so it jumped on the floor and moved
its ass in rhythm like sleeping cities do
waking up in pulsating throbs
to rush hour. And it's
Captain Kangaroo in the morning.
He's all excited and he's jumping—
        up and down
        in and out
        up and down
        in and out—
people running in and out of
revolving doors,
                up and down curbs
trying to stop moving buses
          and you can't stop a moving bus
being driven by Speed Racer.
And the captain got all excited
and he's dropping jellybeans
into speed racers ass
           and k-y is the preferred flavor to cherry

and momma's still singing
open wide your legs oh stainless steel arch
and let that Mississippi flow on out
           first in then out
      then fast now slow
           don't stop God no.
And daddy don't like it,
he's ripping the upholstery of his chair
with his nails, digging the stuffing out
and it's everywhere like confetti
or a chicken hit by a taxi
and daddy's turned on the radio
to drown out mamma's singing.
It's the Hour of Decision with Billy Graham,
while the boys from school are watching
baseball
and its Stan Musial up at bat
strike one
      strike two
          strike three
it's a homer.
Run stan run
run past past mamma biscuits and lava
between the legs of the arch
run like Captain Kangaroo
      up and down, in and out the tall erect building
run like speed racer
run with people eating jellybeans out of my ass
running like the mighty Mississippi flowing with k-y
and the crowd screams for you to run
      and mamma sings louder
      she's going to meet them all in st. louis
all of the screaming fans
screaming because they're dying
screaming because the arch is bleeding between its legs

screaming because they're covered with Mississippi cum
because they're dead ... and so is St. Louis.
It'll all subside soon, the splashing, singing screaming
When I get home the house will be calm.
Daddy will be sleeping in his chair next to the radio
muffled snores and muted static,
Momma sitting on the balcony
silent, scraping the rust from the rails with
her manicured nails
and the St. Louis skyline
is growing dark as the lights go out
now nearly motionless
wet and submerged
beneath the warm rivers of afterglow.

Before God, (an Orchestrated Rebellion in Two Parts)

Part One –

The moon will always see
all that is hidden on Saturday night in the backrooms of the bars,
where heaven is found in the dark
and secrets seep into the slats of wooden floors like spilled seed.
But the moon knows—

        her soft rays

        glide across the room, lick the bodies barely lit

        her light flickers. the rush and recession of pleasure

        that she pours out in tandem and panting.

And I, in the center of the room
a magnolia blossom that has yet to be picked
fleshy, fragrant, fragile
still hidden from the sun like a sin—
lured into languor by the full sensual swoon of this lunar eclipse.

Part Two–

This morning after, the sun is hot,

unforgiving in its judgments

amidst the congregants, clothed in desecration

floral dresses like withered leaves, pressed suits, slacks like verdicts.

It's Sunday morning, and the sun is out for blood, hunting,

        harsh and impervious.

           His light is like a call to war,

             blanketing the room and stifling breath

        until all have conformed to his edicts.

But if you find me, I've shed my mask of floral fragility

emerging a wild weedy warrior

as sacred as I am splintered

fist curled to heaven–

raised in defiance of God's most puerile plans.

January 13, 1985

The St. Louis day
said cement cold gray
and the stinging wind
was stringing Euclid Avenue
into a prism of crystalline lights.
Frozen fingers wooden stubs,
pushed into pants pockets,
fumble numbly for a worn paper
matchbook--
      pull it out.
A straining glance to read
the hastily scrawled
name and number,
a fist, wadding it tight
into a ball--
      then a high pitch.
A good sturdy sling
upwards.
      It filtered
groundward
through
      the
          winter
            wind.

One Hard Night

I feel just like a guest here,
plunged into your chest
like a neckline and
yet cleavaged still.
Our legs were typically limber
in the curl and clutch phase
taut in the tense and release cycles.
I endure patiently, almost laboriously
still lured by that moment
when all my thoughts
would be spangles in light,
sharper than teeth against
flesh.
But you seem to think
that moment may never come
and I am growing content to make do
with our sweat plastered
bodies a trophy to the Marlboro
Man I can't seem to be
for you this time.
So we struggle and groan
trying to force a feel
but end up easing our way
into more frustration
than this will ever be worth.
Passion ebbs,
erection fades, I kick
the sheet off of us and
watch it flutter effortlessly
floorward, draping itself from
the nightstand to the shoes
we had kicked off–
limply, impotently, comfortably.

Still

The glass of vodka seven
is still on the ledge of the sink

where you left it before
you went out in your tight tank top.

I am still sitting
on the lid of the toilet

where I watched you get ready
in front of the bathroom mirror

only now, I am staring at that
half empty glass of vodka seven.

Restless in the Heat

turning from stomach to back
and stomachward again
we were looking for a cool spot
on the sheets
away from the pain
that screamed in your skull
a distant memory of a man
you barely remember
(but i will never forget)
dripped through your sweat
and stuck the sheets
to the back of my thighs
moister still was the silence
so full of wet
i could close my eyes on this
your first year of this pain
of a blue jeaned rough rider
          lying in bed with us
brought
fresh to your mind
i had tasted your perspiration
it was not a new sweat
but i knew my cold hand
could never wipe it dry

Living Crucifixion

Hanging on a cross
not nailed
just hanging.
Flesh not ripped but
splinters in hand.
Struggling twisting writhing
banging my body against
a rough hewn stem.
My choice—
        release the slipping grip
        of my now-wood-scarred hand
        and fall to the abyss
or
        continue to hang on a cross
and learn
that crosses are meant
to die on

Ritual

Skeletons chic now dance
>Your hallowed dance of precision
To perfection/ i hear your steps rattling in unison
Your unskinned bones as they go clicking together
Ann Miller and her ten thousand tapping toes
Skeletons chic now dance
>And let me follow
Gliding across this black tile desert that is
>The sinking sands of time
Skeletons chic now dance
>In the valley of dry bones
We gonna find wat bone dat pelvis is connected to
And i'll pretend i'm dancing with Cyd Charisse
>In the green land of Oz
But wait–
Cyd Charisse didn't dance in Oz and your sharp
Shoulder blades are pointed shoulder pads
Blunt beneath flowing soft chiffon
>Clever deception
You want me to think that there is life
>In your bloodless bones
And that Esther Williams swims amidst fountains
Of milk and honey
>That flow from your breast
But it's all sour
>The maggots and flies have gotten there first
And my beautiful ballerino
>Is a fading memory
>Matted in my pubic hair
Skeletons chic now dance
And I promise I won't mention
Your faces have faded with your skin

The Last Day of Us as a Couple

i had venom for blood
that day

it wasn't

                i didn't love you
                i did so much

it wasn't

                i wanted to break up
                i didn't

but u see
i had an open wound
that had festered years
before u even knew me

& i was finding out

self-hatred would not clot
the flow of blood
that poured out of it

u still came to my party
just to lay ur love and guts right out
across the punch bowl and party plates

i say
        why are you here
u respond with
                just came to see if u were alright

ur sweet gentle lips move
& so i begin to move mine

there was no intent to be cruel
                when i looked you in the face

ur eyes pooled concern
& I wanted to lean
forward
& kiss u

because i wasn't trying to be cruel
but i didn't kiss u

and i did say it
the words
that left my lips

were slow & deliberate
like a knife in u
those words said

                i was fine until you got here

u would take my cruelty
to your grave with u at 26
nearly 7 years after
u forgave me

sometimes at night
i remember u
& then i remember those words
& ur face
i wake up
& feel a pool of blood
beneath me
& i know the wound
has opened again

Where Did the Flowers Go...

The Wise Man Built His House…

I was always taught the house built on love
Would withstand the winds and last a lifetime
I had imagined what we had worked for as indestructible
But there we were watching it crumble
Our little utopia
Like a morning fog nestled on the side of a mountain
Comfortable between the purplish peak
And the rocky base
Like the house built by the foolish man
We knew ours would not last long
Before the sizzling afternoon
Sun scorches it all out as it callously clears everything
Beneath its tormenting gaze.

There is Something Beautiful in a Storm Whether Coming or Going (an elegy for Ken)

Houston's Ash Wednesday floods of 1992
took almost everything you had
except the storm in you.
I saw the remains of it—bold and raw!
Blooming like a rose.
Eye to eye when I first brushed your shoulder,
rounded the bar and circled back.
We ended up at your little condo
on the banks of the White Oak Bayou.

We drank the night like the love we made—
          sweat and sweet skin
and during the next three months,
still in our twenties,
we found our place in the tornado—
an odd paradise of storm- salvaged
appliances and art.
We fucked on the couches and furniture
crowded into your upstairs bedroom,
still pristine despite the bayou water.

One evening,
as rains swept the June heat down,
our second storm was coming up.
You came to get me at the gym,
with important news you said,
and your red mustang convertible was cold,
your eyes were distant and completely black
when you finally spoke with a quiver--
          positive test results,
a clap of thunder and then stunned silence.

The ten-minute drive back to your house
and the rest of the night
took forever.
We found a place to sit on your futon

in the stormy stillness that had engulfed us
and when the rain stopped--
the sunset spread a kaleidoscope
of indigo and orange
streaming through the window blinds of your bedroom.
The rays hit something small,
hanging on your wall in a shadow box—
        a bleeding heart next to a crucifix
you stared and smiled.
With your first words spoken since you delivered the news
"I bought that at DiverseWorks
for $25 dollars"

You were still so proud--
        proud of your art collection
        proud of a bargain.

Then you laid your head on my lap
and closed your eyes.
I fingered your scalp and hair
in a circular motion
as everything began to fall into some sort of chaotic order
between the terrifying storm and the remarkable sky.

We didn't know
The sun was setting on so many things that night.
In the spare of this night-time darkness
we would soon learn that
approaching and departing storms
give witness with alarm and awe
to life's creative cycles–
        the bloom, the beauty, the butchery.

We Are, We Were...Transubstantiation (An Elegy for Ken)

One

our bodies are broken like a sacrament
In the presence of our enemies
I am a pale wafer
so thin beneath my skin
you see the blue
veins that are blood
coursing between your fingers
gripped tight one on each shoulder
you caress me
and–
crack!
I split down the middle
asunder
torn from sternum to sacrum
my separation of left from right
brings your legs above my heart
and my fingers
plunged in the petroleum jelly jar
make their way to the soft spots between your legs
We are now
anointed with oil
one slow push inside
and I can't tell the difference between
you and me anymore
as the ritual destroys
boundaries of place and time
the night restores our soul
until there are no lines to draw
that haven't been dipped
in your spit for a blessing
smudged
as afterglow flickers in the candlelight
dancing like steam off the surface of the still waters outside
our hands, joyfully unwashed
will carry the spirit of this night in scent and sediment

we will lie down in greener pastures
and trust that life, love, or the Lord will keep all of this until...

Two

the morning that brings the sun's glare
is truly the shepherd that nobody wanted

our wine-wet skin and blood-soaked bodies
curdle like a curse
spilling out across the lawn
we are separated by the grass until
I am whole again and you are not
this house of the Lord's where I dwell
is a valley of death
and even though I walk here, I fear everything now
both evil and good
rod and staff
because you are not here and there is no comfort
I am browning like the dry, dusty pages of a hymnal
barren in the back row of a Baptist church
I can't swim upstream
to the open mouth of the river we made
I can't find the table we prepared so carefully
with fruit ripe and swollen
and seeds splayed across your belly like silken cream

I'm trying to find a way back to your lips
before they were split open
before we knew the price this sacrament would demand

In the Three Years I Called You My Lover...(an Elegy for Husaini)

Act 1. We were always up for the party–

We ate dinner at a diner so much
the waiters knew us
So we tricked with one
who lingered far too long at our table
between a grizzled burger
            and a slice of cheesecake.
You loved to dance so we went every single weekend night,
our shirts always sleeveless
                  your jeans always pressed,
and we danced until morning
to Ultra Nate
      or Amber
            or Robin S.
We took trips
      to New Orleans
            and fucked
                  no condoms sometimes
                        with men we didn't yet know.
They danced with us too,
ate with us then followed us to the hotel
like puppies
            with cowboy hats
                  and ripped jeans.

You didn't celebrate Christmas
but since I observed basic Ramadan fasting
you would minimally observe my Christmas.

One Christmas Eve
we went to a dollar store
and bought all of our Christmas
    a tiny tree and tinsel
        cheap gifts and garland
            presents and paper
                a plastic poinsettia.
And we laughed at the bags covering the couch
    then fought over some peach curtains i didn't want
      that you snuck
        to the cashier
And we laughed about the fight after we made up
then hung the curtains and exchanged our gifts

Act 2. We didn't plan for much–

we were too busy really to prepare/even though we always knew
you would leave after you graduated/but to prepare means lists
lists of things to pack and who to contact and where the layover is
the time difference on the other side of the world and who will
pick you up at the airport in Kuala Lumpur/ you just kept saying
"no one stops their life to plan a goodbye."

AIDS was just beginning/and we had to learn how to prepare for it
where to buy condoms/to keep condoms/to have condoms avaiable
to learn where to put them/ how to use them/check expiration
dates/ to be good hosts for the cowboys we brought home or when
we just wanted to fuck/ so we had some in the nightstand and
some in the silverware drawer/because spontaneity was important
to you/

so there was plenty to do but there were no lists of it all/no record
of it and then you left early at 6 am while I slept/you didn't even
wake me I was completely unprepared for an unspoken goodbye/
to sleep alone for how big the house suddenly felt/unprepared to
go to the diner alone to fuck alone with strangers/you left the tiny
tree in the living room closet next to the poinsettia/the condoms
were still in the silverware drawer and I wasn't prepared for how
cold Christmas could be/

in time I adjusted to your being gone and took the peach curtains
down/

Act 3. The world comes back around –

Twenty years later, we connect again
when I finally see your Facebook alert.
We arrange a call in the morning at seven
on a September day, driving to work.

I breeze past a flock of purple martins,
clustering, enroute south from colder fronts.
Your voice sounds cheerful as you start in
about husbands, work and then once

we get to old friends to see who's still alive,
it begs the question of status and health.
"I am good" I say "somehow I survived?"
Then a long pause and a shorter breath

"I'm taking care of my lover with AIDS"
In my head, I can fill in the spaces.

Act 4. Closure?–

A few years after,
On your birthday,
At the beginning
Of the second pandemic
I've lived through,
With the sun peeking through tree branches
And the first rose on my rose bush
Still in its bud
I get a text message
From Shafinaz your niece in Malaysia
Saying "Before he died he asked me
To tell you how much he loved you"

And once again
You have left me—
        Completely unprepared

**The Things I Can't Forget, Things I Can't Keep
(an Elegy for Joe)**

If I could have read your body like a work of art
Left to right or right to left
Maybe up and down
Or just start in the center
Splat
Beneath your navel
And work outward
Massaging your skin
With my tongue
Collecting the sweet sweat
And slight hairs that get caught between my teeth
If I could deconstruct you like a Picasso
Arms and neck nape
Glutes and toes
Then lips as I inhaled the smell of your skin
The lotion you applied below your knees
I yearn to hear your gentle voice again
To feel your unshaven cheek on my jawline
Below my chin
Or to reach around your shoulders
And rock you like a wave
Until our minds break against the shore
And we are lowered gently
Into the palm of the artist

The Things That Are Held in the Heart of the Earth
(an Elegy for Michael)

If I dig a well deep enough,
I know I will strike something—
crystal clear water pure or crude thick oil—
coarse and sludging up.
Since the core of the earth is erratic
and as I am a product of its dust and mud,
I am erratic too—
asymmetrical without balance.
Though my surface is lush meadows
laid across rolling green hills,
serene as a sunset on a warm summer day.
please, look closer—
beneath the blanket of bramble and grass
raveled in a tangle of root and rhizome.
See how the soft soil absorbs
the gentle quake of a grieving heart.

After You Died I Drove to New Orleans to Hide (for Ken)

One
It's not the first time i've been here/
I like it because of the scarcity of light/
I like it because you have never been here/
because here i can bask in anonymity
and alcohol/allowing the alcohol/ smooth/
          and shimmering in its glass to sooth the pain
of the anonymity that i am loving/ the pain
in my mind is transferred to my gut with
slippery fingers grabbing my intestines tight/
catching & yanking & wrenching & releasing/
like a farmer milking the dry udder of a cow.

Two

A live band plays & the cornet/
catching & releasing what little
light there is in the room/
is like a balm on the wound/
alternately sharpening my focus like a
razor strap then loosening it into a
blurry mush/
a man at another table draws my
stare/ a black turtleneck in june
and he's telling some story that no one
in his party seems the least bit concerned
with/he's thrashing his arms around/
ribbons in the wind punctuating
nothing/ but maybe too wildly
because his hand just hit his drink/

Three
Through a thick wash of vodka   the glass slides off the table/
performs an amazing
                    triple somersault backwards nose-dive/
radiating like neon the dim light from
its slick back/
smashing
into
the
floor/
it   takes   the   impact   of   the   tile   with   a
large   splash
of alcohol and glass/   millions of minute shards
                    darting in different directions/
        catching
                    and
                    releasing
what little light there is in the room /
        they lay silently on the floor
                    sparkling like tiny crystal prisms
off of their jagged menacing edges/

An Elegy for Joe Perez

It was a Saturday night
And I spent many of them here
At a hospice
Tonight I was in room 6
With you

I didn't know you
Had never met you
But imagined that once
You were a handsome man
Dark eyes and square jaw

No longer able to speak
You reached out your hand
I heard your eyes say
"Please don't go"
So I just stared back

In that moment I lost all words
So I squeezed your hand
And my grip said
"It's okay to go"
And that night you heard me
And that night you did

I can only hope I helped
With that decision

When We Were Vampires at Night (an Elegy for Michael)

A scrim of black and gray
Clouds my memory
Like a midnight graveyard
We are the two naked shadows
That disappear into a mist
A mist that beads
On the nape of your neck
Back of your thighs
Drizzling onto my tongue
Like wine into a chalice
Like sin on my lips
Wet like precum
Precursor to pleasure
Those late evenings sneaking into
The religion center on campus
Fucking in the empty confessionals
   In the small second-floor chapel
Bodies fully crucified and fully risen
A sacrifice laid out on an altar
Of sacred flesh
Dipped in sin and our crimson DNA
Your pores oozing pleasure
Profane with perspiration
Desire in small salty drops
And then in one feral moment
I pull your body hair from between my lips
Like I'd pull the pit from the meat of a peach
And relish still the secretions
Dripping like blood from my chin to my forearm
This is how life gives
The sweet and savory
In droplets like blood
In separate moments
Of rush and retreat
And I still feel your presence
As real and wet
As a pool of blood

As distant and drifting
As a wine stain on satin choir robe

The Things That God Holds Above Us (an Elegy for Michael)

I've been looking at this gray
For endless days
But the rain won't come
Even the blackbirds are circling the sky
Pacing like bored school children waiting for recess
And like those birds, you want to go I know,
Drift upward
Heaven bent
On some final journey
As we have been taught the soul does
When the body dies.

I've spent the years since you died
Trying to steel myself
      So I don't have to let go.
Like the great tailed grackles that
      Circle and circle the clouds
In ceaseless search for a solution.
Are they waiting for the rain?
Or just a break from the gray
Where they can dive up into the blue
That must feel bottomless to them
Because it has no end,
No floor above.

I am like those black birds that can't give up.
Searching for a break in my memory
Some new recollection of an old fact
      That shoots up like a geyser
To connect the fragmented dots.
I still hear the pitch of your voice, elegant, reserved
But the words
That streamed out like a fragile butterfly
      Are gone completely.
Night winds still carry the faint smell of the lotion
You applied to your stomach
      Where I pressed my face in a kiss

But your expressions of pleasure fall as silent
As a suburban street at midnight.

As the world moves on
      To more effective therapies,
      To new pandemics,
I worry that if I forget, the world will forget

And I can't keep looking at
This overcast sky,
Trying to reoccupy
Some twinkling juncture of time
Huddled in the stairwell of the university
         Escaping a midnight rain
         Eating with fingers from a jar of spaghetti
Or naked under your dorm bed,
Hiding from your roommate
Licking the sweat off the same fingers that earlier fed me.
These memories have had so many years
To do what memories do,
To fly up into a cover of clouds and slowly disintegrate.
It's like trying to hold steam
Or watching my mouth exhale in December.
Knowing that this visible release of air,
Tangible only for moments
Has seconds before complete atmospheric dissolution.

Some things that can't be held

Some things that don't last/ Are still real.
I watched your spirit, like a beautiful blackbird,
     Strong and shattered, resolute as it surrendered
And slipped through hospice sheets and dull white curtains,
Drifting up, borne on the breeze
Searching for solace,
Shambling skyward.
A Greek chorus of ache and supplication
That finally bounced off
God's deaf ear
     And floated away,
Disappearing in smoky filaments of fading breath.

An Elegy for the Lover Who Isn't Dead

It may have been only three months
Sometimes the fires that burn the brightest
Are the shortest and can't sustain the heat

Let it Sleep (An Elegy for Michael)

moving into the dark that is night
into black that is you
that is delicious
i release myself high
on the dull glow of your fading skin
our searching legs rearrange
to recapture the slow sensual spirits
of a sleeping sun
that's turned his head low upon your pillow
to cast his hot breath on you
sighs flowing with the dark into night
      a full moon eclipsing lightly
      between your fingers

I Step Over Magnolia Blossoms When They Have Fallen to the Ground
(an Elegy for Michael)

I can't walk under the fragrant shadow
Of a magnolia tree and look at those plush,
pale blossoms, soft and fluttering in the breeze,
without hearing your voice in my ear.

A sound still as silky and scented
As an entire forest of evergreen or Viburnum davidii.
Your voice is Mississippi to me.
Playful as a picnic,
Delicate like a thin cotton t-shirt
        In the hot, humid sun.
A drawl as thick as an arboretum of pinetum,
        Yet a timbre so brittle
        It could blow away in the wind
            Like the sandy soil that covers the shaded ground.

I've tried to hold your memories close
but life moves on.
And that massive river
        Has pushed against every boundary we had.
                It has trampled every fertile place.
                    It would wash away those trees
In its unrelenting rush of muddy water–
                        If I would allow it.

But today, I'm in Houston
Sitting on a porch swing
On a hot September day
I'm fighting off the
Rush of that river
Against an embankment of memories
Like Texas holds onto its heat,
Wrestling with the cooler fronts of autumn.

A lemonade in hand,
Looking at that majestic magnolia grandiflora,
I watch the petals
Of the delicate sweet flower
That have fallen
Onto the sidewalk,
Turn brown in the afternoon sun.

You Gave Them To Me in My Hand (An Elegy for Ken)

one summer afternoon we rolled
around on the hill we jokingly called
the grassy knoll in downtown Houston
you picked a flower fragile
and in the tussle
it immediately lost
all of its light purple petals
i watched them float off the stem groundward
paste to the perspiration on the flesh
of your white and freckled shoulders
the heat was as heavy in the air
as the musk of grass and sweat that surrounded us
like a potpourri of naked bodies and clover leaves
wedged in your pubic hair

we were young, still in college
and we didn't have two of anything in those days
so we gave each other what we could
and what we could give was all we had...
the smells
              stray blades of grass
              and clover leaves
                    purple flower petals
                        the hair and the skin

these were your gifts to me
for my fingers to feel
my tongue to taste
to get stuck in the back of my throat
or just tickling my nose
you gave me those things
and that afternoon I became a rich man
counted in mindfulness and experiences

we didn't know then
you had given all you could
and would not live long enough
to give any more

and I didn't know then
that I would never live long enough
to spend the currency of memories we had amassed

This is for When I Crave the Smell of Moist Soil (An Elegy for Tracy Karl Silverberg)

the glint of a black orchid that blooms in your eyes
and hangs above my head like the shiny leather straps
crossing your chest
                    isn't real
neither is the white horse
soft as velvet to the touch
that grazes the hairs on your lower back
like it was a dewy meadow in the early morning
                    of an august summer day
the pervasive drumbeat of Texas heat
that drives a fire of sweat and lips
onto the muddy ground—
                    tongue and torch—
is all spirit now
the dirt on our faces and hands
joyful like child's play
                    is phantom
the salty taste of your arm pit
or slick razor strap feel of spit on your skin
                    is all fantasy
we are both ready for it/the tumbledown through tree branches
              onto the warm soft grass
the impending chaos of thrust and breath/the splash in the puddle
                    ending in one long exhale
sinking into a soft wet silence
all of this will soon be buried in the earth
beneath the gravel and grave markers
with the rainworms and horned beetles
alongside the weed roots
                  i will never come back here again
                  for the rain has blurred my reality
                  and all our borders have been transgressed

Our Last Date Before You Died
(an Elegy for Ken)

On the last day that i saw you,
we had spent the entire day
on the west side of town visiting
art galleries. You loved the stern
vibrations of well-planned order
white walls and shellacked concrete floors.
You were driven by your hunger and pride,
your need to love art and to understand it, to give in to it
and to give it to me.
At one exhibit, you stopped,
gazing closely at an abstract painting
of the ocean, a seashore, a sunny sky and sandy beach.
You reached out your finger
and gently touched the piece.
"Ken" I exclaimed!
You grabbed my hand and placed it on the painting,
"Feel how smooth that is".
The movement of a long wave
captured by a smooth brush stroke
punctuated by a sharp point of acrylic,
dabbled at the crest of the wave—
tactile and visual.
We would never go there,
you would never see any beach again.
"Boys" a voice from behind the desk would shout.
My hand went quickly into my pocket
while yours didn't move.
You were lost in this world, this fragmented landscape.
These brush strokes and splotches
offered you something that I couldn't offer anymore.
And for the first time since I had met you,
I was outside of where you were.

I could feel this painting with my finger
but I couldn't be in the sand and sea with you.
I looked apologetically at the woman behind the desk
and then I looked at you.
Where we were standing
        felt like a languid, protracted stretch on a sunny beach.
Where we were going
        felt like a dive into a cold dark ocean.
                        From which you would never surface.

The Apples Have Fallen From the Tree...

Mom and Dad

I've looked for you around street corners
In the sidewalks of the cities I've lived in
In the dark crevices of cheap apartments
And in suitcases I've packed to travel

In your death I feel I have found you both
Free of ego's curse and creeping watch
I feel your soul in small ways now
Sitting on a porch swing coffee in hand

Or just waiting for a clean wash of rain
From a distant storm marked by black clouds
An irreverent gust of warm wet winds
Then thunder and a sweet smell of petrichor

       I feel you now in the cross-country drive
       Down a long windy Missouri two-lane

**A Room with No Doors (an elegy in 5 parts for my father–
The Rev. Denver Moore)**

The DreamScape

All the walls are white,
Naked in front of the bathroom mirror
In this light so bright I couldn't
Hide a pimple on my ass.
I brace myself
Then a kyphotic plunge forward into the glass.

Forehead first
And it's hard,
It separates like fractured liquid,
Red diamonds bold against a black film lit like stars.
Tiny gemstones, rubies, or blue emeralds.
They snake and swirl,
Puddle and pool,
In some dreams you can see clearly and when I can–
Oh my god this is blood!
It is dense and falling in large drops.
Maniacal, winking with the curves and then
Taunting me with a slash.
And it keeps falling heavy like the crimson sunset outside
And then drips again
Over my bones and under my skin like plastic wrap.

The river that streams
From you on the couch
To me at six years old
Lying on my belly
In the middle of the living room floor.

Innocence and Betrayal

In pajamas, playing with my United States puzzle,
I place the last piece left on the floor–Missouri–
Perfectly into the center of the puzzle.
It is red, the color of a heartbeat–
As if colored by our blood.
I look up at you on the couch watching me
And I feel your pride
Pumping under your shirt.

Do you see my veins laid open
Next to yours and the blue and scarlet
That flows between us and around.

I place my hand,
The same one that found the puzzle piece,
Onto your hospital gown
And pull it over your shoulder to keep you warm.
Your skin is thin veins and purple spiders like bugs.
The hum and beep of machines against silence
Is a current, a rushing liquid.

And I can only ask–
How did we get from there to here?
From the living room floor to the hospital bed
What happened in the years in between?

From your carpeted podium,
A preacher with a pulpit,
Where you stood like a lion in a suit.
Your voice never quiet. Always loud, bellowing,
The timbre, the tone. Always up in my face like a fist,
A judgement as bold as it was calloused.

The Hospital and Coma

And now you are a frail ringleader
In a your medically induced circus.
And you haven't spoken in weeks,
Not a single word
And not just you, nobody speaks.
It's so quiet in this room–
My mother and family, even the doctors are silent.
As if your secrets were theirs to protect.
The nurses change bedpans and gown, swab your mouth,
Constantly in and out–but silent.
They hold their thermometers and blood pressure cuffs quietly,
As quietly as you held onto your other life for so many years.

So, after all of what we have been through as a father and son,
It's come down to this—
The bright white lights,
The black hole behind the mirror
The deafening "shhhh" of it all.

Where Did You Go

In your current state,
I can't ask you how you spent your summer afternoons,
Curled up in a sunroom with another married man,
Maybe listening to Fleetwood Mac on the radio
As sunlight filtered through wooden blinds.
Or were they spent like my summers
In the dirty bathrooms of Forest Park.
Making furtive eye contact with the college soccer players,
Their muscular legs shining with sweat and smudges of dirt
From the nearby fields.
All I know is
The dirty bathrooms and soccer players,
The married men and the radio
Became secrets,
To do what secrets do,
to wound, to worsen, to rile and rift.
Like the secrets I've kept from you.

The Sound of Reality

And when I finally open my eyes,
Red and sore like a door to this world
That you're drifting through.
I am awake now
Torn in half, but awake.
A puzzle piece that has slidden into a grooved slot
Between the lifelong secrets that unite us,
And the calloused dogma that has separated us.
Here in the bathroom
Leaning on the sink,
Amidst the sparkling shards of crystal and tainted blood,
I see your reflection in this mosaic.
The trinity you've carefully curated for most of your life
A proud father watching his child but only from a distance,
A man who lived behind a glass darkly,
The ghostly shell that is now the personification of your secrets.

Kinder Than the Man (an Elegy for my Mother)

As darkness falls like coffee,
Spilling itself across this lazy St. Louis sky–
the moon also rises, reporting for third shift work.
There was really never a man in moon–
It's always been a woman.
I've seen her face clearly
and through the years
I have learned to rely on her consistent wink and seductive smile.
I just could never let her out
because I never knew the purpose she served–
that is, I never knew it until the night you died.

And tonight she is peeking through the shadow of her waxing
gibbous,
a bright satin dream under sheets of dark clouds,
a courtesan whose arms are soft, caressing
like streams of violet gauze.
She reaches for me
letting down her hair
until I am wrapped in cream and cotton.
She will pull me out of this barren white room
and into her womb–

A Halloween many years ago,
where you are helping me with my costume for the night
as I try on your dresses and heels,
an off- the -shoulder top and peasant skirt,
and we fall on the bed laughing

until my belly hurts.

But now the joy
and spontaneity of those days
eludes us as we settle
into a more subdued bond
my head is resting
securely on your breast

where I can enjoy
the comforting smell of face powder and perfume.
As I hold your hand for one last moment,
I finally see God and it's not what or who I thought.
God is a woman.
Fanning out across the clouds in wanton repose,
she weaves her lustrous rays
like a silken fabric over this sleeping city.
God isn't lurking in the darkness behind this lunar eclipse,
—no—
God is the workin' girl waiting for quittin' time,
cleaning toilets and stocking supply closets.
God is the waitress on graveyard duty,
barking out orders and spindling tickets,
slinging hash and refilling coffee.

She carries salvation out of the kitchen
on plates of meatloaf and mashed potatoes,
she heals the hurting with heaping portions
of biscuits ladled with gravy.
And her infallible word?
It is a soft and gentle lullaby
sung in a whispered tone illuminated
by a streetlamp through a crevice cut into the curtains.

But dusk is signaling a shift change
and I am intensely watching you
fall into this sunset
faster than I had ever thought possible.
I don't know if you are ready to go
but the beep of your machine is beginning to flatten
into one thin green line.
And the walls of this room are starting to heave
in tandem with your shallow gasps for air,
then with the force of your very last breath
you caress the palm of my hand—

and I am once again lowered like an empty bucket
to bathe in your well filled with milk.

Echoes Will Bloom...

When Life Offers a Healing...

Stand naked in the rain
Arms spread wide
And embrace if you can
The dark and clap
Of thunder and clouds
Even the grief of lost love
Behind all of this
   You might find
The lightning spark of new love
The joy of a child born
And you will feel your soul
Through your open palms
Dive up
Forward of a far-flung flicker
A fractal of your fragile fate
Feel the voltage electrify intensify
Then unify
Then maybe
     Just maybe
The comfort you find
Is in your conversation

Under the clouds
   Amidst this anger wind and sky
You are finally talking with God
   And they are talking back

The Disturbing Tale of the Dancing Pig (A Tribute to Kenny Joe Spivey)

sometimes early in the morning
just before the sun comes up
a pig will pop his head up out of the mud
slop and shit dripping from his snout
then he drops low and rolls around, squirms and wiggles his ass
before he's off and under the mud again

sometimes a pig dances like a gentleman
dressed best in breeches and waistcoat
pinker skin and more pristine than any other callers

but that doesn't mean the courtesan
would dance with him for a drink
he offers a gallant arm to the corseted beauty
bent at the elbow with a slight
inclined bow at the hips to show respect

and she still kicks him with her boot
and pushes him away
how much more finesse does he need
how much more grace
does it take to make his arms
look elegant and longer than his belly

to make his chortling snort sound like sweet nothings

a pig has to be so much more in life
a pig has to be the parent who goes to all the PTA meetings
or the driver who never forgets to signals at lane changes
or the lover who makes coffee after everyone else cums

pigs have to do all that
and they still won't get half the respect
of the guy who just cut the line at the supermarket

he's in a hurry

because his wife is waiting in the Lexus
and he has to pick up his step kids
at a ball game.

he looks at me like i've got
his shit
all over me
i'm not bothered so i smile and nod
because each day at dawn the pigs dance free
i know
i dance with them

The Fog Lies Against the Horizon

You move through me
Like an early morning fog
Your wet lips
Like the dew
Lightly brush my nipples
You lie over me
Like a warm noonday sky
And the smell of your love
Like a honeysuckle
Blowing in the breeze
Of your hot breath down my back
My eyes close tight
As the sunset rises in your eyes
My arms span across the horizon
To embrace the coming
        nightfall

Last Night

I reach out
my arms
Full of
     You
Are still
     Empty
We are
Full of
     N
     I
      G
      H
       T
        F
       A
       L
        L
Nightfall is heartbreak
I can feel the words
Of your mother
Start to pour
Like tears from your eyes.
I
     Am
        So
           Sorry

At Work

I've sat in this small gray padded box
Called an office cubicle
I look at my hands, feet
Remember your sweet cheek
Pressed warm against my shoulder
Or my chin
In this sterile place
Where you have never been or seen
I am miles from you
I imagine you at home
Wrapped in a white sheet
My pillow close to your chest
I need you
        More than before
My eyes are wide open
Love is never blind

Is This How You Settle Down

I am settling like an old house
Wilder days melting like ice
But a frozen foundation nonetheless
Which I feel content to rest upon
Yet your youthful innocence and yearning
Strains us beyond our room
I know what causes you pain
I know what contents me

Zoom Therapy

You're the five naked faces behind
The little boxes
You're the real talking heads in my life
But you are also the place i go
When I need
To empty out my mind
Like it was a bottle of spoiled milk
To wash down the kitchen drain
      And rinse away the curdled clots
So I can refill it
Like it was a pitcher of homemade horchata
          Velvety and sweet
          Real cream and cinnamon
     Or a wine carafe
Full of Jesus' transformed miracle water
That I can savor in my mind
     On my tongue
     Until I'm overflowing with value and veneration

Traces

the night sky is a plush bed
of purple and red
this dark velvet cover
pierced by stars overhead

we spent that first summer
like kids to discover
the world at our heels
as if we could outrun her

those youthful ideals
conversation reveals
a loftier place
that our struggle conceals

the breeze with the trace
of your lips on my face
as I lie in this space
of your gentle embrace

It Is All I Have Left at the End of the Day
(for Emerson)

Finally, a father at fifty.
Fatigued and fillipped by choices I've made,
Walking through hallways,
Turning off lights and picking up toys.
You are mine now nine,
Scared of the dark when alone,
You sleep in my bed most nights.
Without waking you,
I replace the sheets under you
And a clean pad.
Your heartbeat is gentle
As you explore the safe spaces in your dreams.
They bubble up like the joy I feel and drool out over your pillow.
I turn off the lamp and sit
In the dark for a moment,
I watch the ghosts that still live in my brain
Suspended in the stillness—
      Lovers gone to AIDS
           Their lips still brush the side of my neck,
    High school bullies' terrifying taunts
          Hurled in tight jeans,
    A fervent Sunday School teacher's brimstone
          Targeted to a timid twelve year old—
As they try to do what they've always done,
Incite my doubts and stroke my fears,
I can feel my mask and the years it took to make
Disintegrate like Kool-Aid in water.
I exhale—
You can help me now. I am no longer afraid.

You and I: A Poem for my Son

after William Carlos Williams

"The bond we have"
Was your opening line and
how your heart first fell out of your
little red hoodie
onto the white paper
like a wheelbarrow
next to the fluffy chicks–
                    tipped.

And my heart
was in my eyes
as I watched you, now
glazed with tear-water
beside the pencil scratches
and title—
                    "Me & You: A Poem for my Dad."

As I read your words
through your eyes,
I could feel
in my chest my heartbeat
whispering–

                    "My son wrote a poem."

Today I'm Dad

Amid the smell of the breakfast I am cooking
Through the jeans I'm wearing
That are too tight
For a Saturday morning,
I find my husband asleep
In his easy chair and my teen-ager
   He won't wake up for a few hours.
I can be annoyed or I can go get donuts
Because I have a choice
Because
Like you always say–
   Some dads do that for their kids
   And today—I'm THAT Dad.

March 22nd, 2025

Sometimes late in
March, an overworked
dead rhyme like
sing and spring
will come to life
again when
the first red cardinal chirps
to the humming of a
window fan, the rattling
of the papers it
blows around the
room or the burring
of the neighbor's
lawn mower drumming
through the whirring
blades, form an
ad hoc jazz quartet
and together they
all sing spring

Can a Pig Just be Free (the Pigs Dance II)
A celebration of the life of Kenny Joe Spivey

it's dusk
and just before bedtime
a pig loves to pop
his head up
out of the mud and slop
shit dripping from snout to hoof
wiggle his ass and dance
and tonight its disco
glittery pants stretched
over pink bellies
afro wigs with
hairy ears popping out
between tight curls
and those platform hooves
that help him teeter across the floor

it's a swine soiree
a real oinker orgy
and the pig is just enjoying
the night
but even tho he has finesse
it is hidden behind his distended gut
lost amidst the chortles and grunts.
if you don't understand
this innocent gathering of pork
it looks too much like a porcine playground
and that is a threat
a threat to
the men in suits that won't get their
cufflinks dirty.

it's the man in the supermarket
here he comes again
dressed sharply in his J Crew
but still more fetid than the last time I saw him
just cut the line because he feels
entitled to do that
after all his wife is waiting in the car

and he has to pick his kids up at soccer practice

when he turns to look at me
I know what he sees
he thinks his shit is dripping off
my snout
and he has to pass a law, I guess
he thinks he has a mandate

but does he?
is there a mandate over a pig's rights.
can anyone even claim that?
because there will always be pigs
and they will always show up in your streets and schools and
churches
and I would rather join their orgy
       because every morning at dawn
           disco, waltz, or polka
      the pigs still dance free

Acknowledgments

To Ntazoke Shange, you were the first, the person who lit the fire. You taught me that poetry can be what I need to be and that my voice matters.

To the teachers who followed: Linda Gregg, your personality and charm were matched only by the care you showed your students. Pattyann Rogers, we seemed to spar more than we meshed, but you taught me restraint and beauty.

To CLI, the wonderful staff, and instructors; Hiram, your vision is inspiring. Lisa Montagne, thank you for poetry church. That was the highlight of my week for a year. Margaret Elysia Garcia, thank you for your wisdom and gentle guidance. You inspired me to get my first poem published.

To the Daxson Publishing team, Erica and Cherice: Thank you for your belief in me and your support.

To the Pace Team: Assim, you gave me the platform to jump back into this thing and reignite a poetry fire.

Elisabeth, I first began calling myself a "poet" while in your group.

Dearest Jessica, Shelley, Stephanie, Lori, and Kerry, you all gave me the push I needed on multiple occasions to get this done and you always believed I could do it.

Justine Jannise, your expert writing prompts are on display multiple times throughout this collection. Thank you for your thoroughness and attention to detail.

My gratitude to the following publications in which these poems originally appeared, often in altered form:

Beyond Queer Words: A Queer Anthology—"This Is For When I crave the Smell of Moist Soil (An Elegy for Tracy Karl)"

screendoorreview.com–"The Spot We've Cleared in the Weeds (An Elegy for Ken)" stoneofmadnesspress.com– "The Disturbing Tale of the Dancing Pig"

powderspress.com– "The Things That Are Held in the Heart of the Earth (An Elegy for Michael)"

2024. Edited by Hiram Sims, First Edition ed., My First Trip to the Library, World Stage Press, 2024, pp. 70–71.

About the Author

Scott Moore is a husband, father, and queer poet from Houston, TX. His work explores the intersectionality of LGBTQIA+ life in modern society. His poems have appeared in *Beyond Queer Words: A Queer Anthology*, powderspress.com, screendoorreview.com, and stoneofmadnesspress.com.

Publisher's Note

Daxson publishing was created to help marginalized artists and their allies publish their work, so the world can hear their voice. The vision for this publishing house is to help people get their work out there, and not have them struggle finding their way through the publishing process. Everyone's voice deserves to be heard, and we are here to help. If you are interested in submitting a manuscript, email daxsonpublishing@gmail.com.
Support our cause! Buy our books at daxsonpublishing.com.